Self-Love Journal

Written By: Rashanda Crisp

SELF-LOVE JOURNAL

DEDICATION

This journal is dedicated to every Queen that walked through the fire and came out with beautiful scars.

INTRODUCTION

Self-love creates the foundation that provides the
ability to discern who and what you allow into your
life.
This is your personal self-love journal, created to
help you create ways to fill yourself with positive
thoughts, visualize your goals and to normalize
putting yourself first.
Most importantly you will be encouraged to look
deep within and challenge yourself to create the life
that you deserve.

Journal Instructions

For the next four weeks one day at a time
begin your journey of acceptance and clarity. Your
self-love journal begins with fourteen days of
reflection, followed by fourteen days of journaling.
Each day you will take time out for yourself to
connect with your thoughts, goals, and desires. The
final step in this process is to write a letter of love
and forgiveness to yourself.
To heal from any wound, we must acknowledge it,
treat it, and be patient while it heals.
Today you are beginning your journey towards
healing your wounds.

Complete each day by being honest with yourself;
Unapologetically!

DAY 1

I AM MENTALLY...

DAY 2

I AM EMTIONALLY...

DAY 3

I AM PHYSICALLY…

DAY 4

I AM LACKING...

DAY 5

I FEEL INSECURE WHEN…

DAY 6

I FEEL OVERWHELMED WHEN…

DAY 7

I AM IN NEED OF…

DAY 8

I AM UNSURE OF…

DAY 9

THE THINGS I AM GRATEFUL FOR ARE…

DAY 10

MY BIGGEST CHALLENGE IS…

DAY 11

I AM DETERMINED TO…

DAY 12

I NEED TO MAKE MORE TIME FOR…

DAY 13

MY BIGGEST FEAR IS...

DAY 14

I AM MOST CONTENT WHEN...

WEEK 3- BEGIN JOURNALING

DAY 15-28

DAILY AFFIRMATIONS

EXPRESS POSITIVE THOUGHTS OR IDEAS.

DAILY EXPRESSIONS

YOUR THOUGHTS OR MOOD

DAILY GOALS

LIST THINGS THAT YOU ACCOMPLISHED TODAY.

LIST ONE THING YOU CAN FORGIVE YOURSELF FOR TODAY.

DISCOVERY

LIST ONE THING YOU THAT YOU HAVE DISCOVERED ABOUT YOURSELF.

DAILY HEALTH GOAL

LIST WAYS TO IMPROVE YOUR HEALTH.

DAILY RELEASE

LIST ONE THING THAT YOU ARE READY TO RELEASE.

DAILY PRAYER

LIST A PRAYER THAT BRINGS YOU PEACE.

ACCEPTANCE

LIST THINGS THAT ARE OUT OF YOUR CONTROL.

CREATE YOUR MOOD

WITHIN THE NEXT YEAR I WILL..

TODAY I HAVE ACHIEVED..

LIST HEALTHY BOUNDARIES THAT YOU CAN ENFORCE.

CONGRATULATIONS!

YOU HAVE SUCCESSFULLY COMPLETED YOUR
SELF-LOVE JOURNAL.

ON THE FOLLOWING PAGES WRITE A LETTER
TO THE PERSON YOU HAVE NOW DISCOVERED
WITHIN YOURSELF. INCLUDE WHY YOU
DESERVE TO BE LOVED,
AND THE IMPORTANCE OF SELF-LOVE.

SPEAK LIFE INTO YOURSELF AND BE PROUD
THAT FOR THE PAST FOUR WEEKS YOU TOOK
TIME OUT DAILY TO HEAL THE PARTS OF YOU
THAT WERE BROKEN.

XOXO

DEAR QUEEN,

Made in the USA
Las Vegas, NV
20 October 2023

79358111R00022